D1529782

STEM Jobs
with Cars

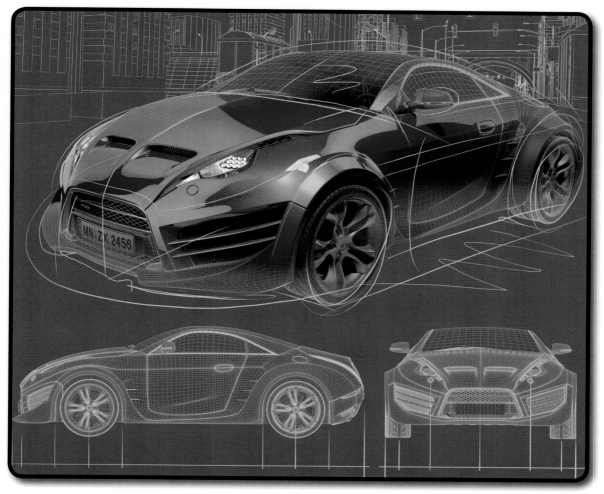

Jane Katirgis

rourkeeducationalmedia.com

Scan for Related Titles
and Teacher Resources

Before Reading:

Building Academic Vocabulary and Background Knowledge

Before reading a book, it is important to tap into what your child or students already know about the topic. This will help them develop their vocabulary, increase their reading comprehension, and make connections across the curriculum.

1. *Look at the cover of the book. What will this book be about?*
2. *What do you already know about the topic?*
3. *Let's study the Table of Contents. What will you learn about in the book's chapters?*
4. *What would you like to learn about this topic? Do you think you might learn about it from this book? Why or why not?*
5. *Use a reading journal to write about your knowledge of this topic. Record what you already know about the topic and what you hope to learn about the topic.*
6. *Read the book.*
7. *In your reading journal, record what you learned about the topic and your response to the book.*
8. *After reading the book complete the activities below.*

Content Area Vocabulary
Read the list. What do these words mean?

blueprint
data
exponent
features
GPS
green
hybrid cars
lasers
molecules
reconstruction
simulations
spoiler

After Reading:

Comprehension and Extension Activity

After reading the book, work on the following questions with your child or students in order to check their level of reading comprehension and content mastery.

1. *Describe the role of STEM in the car industry. (Summarize)*
2. *Why do engineers make improvements to new cars? (Infer)*
3. *What subjects would you need to study to create new biofuels? (Text to self connection)*
4. *What new technology might you expect to see in future cars? (Infer)*
5. *Describe how computer animation helps people analyze a car crash. (Visualize)*

Extension Activity

Draw a picture of a futuristic car with new technology and improvements never before seen. Label each improvement with the field of study necessary to make it a reality.

Table of Contents

What Is STEM?

Self-driving cars, NASCAR racetracks, safer airbags . . . What do these things have in common? Scientists, mathematicians, and engineers are the brains behind these and many other car technologies. And all their jobs require a STEM education. STEM is a shortcut for talking about science, technology, engineering, and mathematics.

What does STEM stand for?

Science
Technology
Engineering
Mathematics

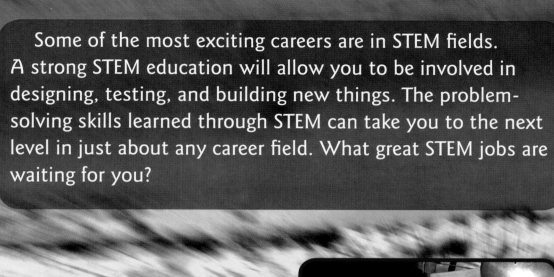

Some of the most exciting careers are in STEM fields. A strong STEM education will allow you to be involved in designing, testing, and building new things. The problem-solving skills learned through STEM can take you to the next level in just about any career field. What great STEM jobs are waiting for you?

Car engineers combine their love of math and science with their interest in automobiles.

STEM on the Motor Speedway

Engineering does not get much faster or thrilling than at the racecar speedway. NASCAR teams hire up to forty engineers to build and race a winning car. They test designs and engines that can shave milliseconds off a racer's time.

A NASCAR team's lead race engineer is one of the top positions. In the car shop, they study computer models and past racing results to improve a car's performance. They place a car in a wind tunnel to study how the car's shape affects air drag. It is like one long science experiment, using math, physics, and mechanical engineering.

A car's computer can tell the engineer how well it performed during a race.

NASCAR engineers fine tune each car to perform its best during a race.

STEM in Action!

The Daytona 500 is one of the highlights of the NASCAR season. It is a 500-mile race. The track is 2.5 miles long.

How many laps does a NASCAR driver complete to finish the Daytona 500?

500 miles ÷ 2.5 miles per lap = 200 laps

In 2013, Jimmie Johnson won the Daytona 500 in about 3 hours, 8 minutes. What was the average speed, in miles per hour, of his winning car?

Use a calculator to convert 8 minutes into a decimal:
8 minutes divided by 60 minutes in an hour = 0.14
Add 0.14 to 3 hours. His race time was 3.14 hours

500 miles ÷ 3.14 hours = 159.24 miles per hour

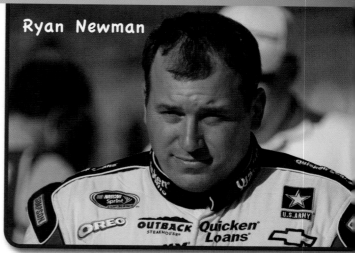
Ryan Newman

Some NASCAR drivers are also scientists! Ryan Newman was always good at math and physics, and today uses them to win. He has combined his engineering degree with his love of racecar driving.

In his laboratory, the car shop, Ryan works with other engineers. They ready the car for all race situations, such as making sure the tires will grip when he is racing at 200 miles per hour (322 kilometers per hour). Ryan says, "Racing is one big huge equation." Any variable can turn a perfect race into a disaster!

All of Ryan Newman's hard work pays off on the race track.

Real STEM Job: *NASCAR Engineer*

Each year, NASCAR engineers think about changes they can make to the racecars that will help their team win during the coming season. For 2014, engineers wanted to learn how changes in design could allow the cars to race closer together. They also wanted to find ways to lessen the draft created by a lead car. A car at the front blocks airflow for the cars behind it, allowing them to gain more speed.

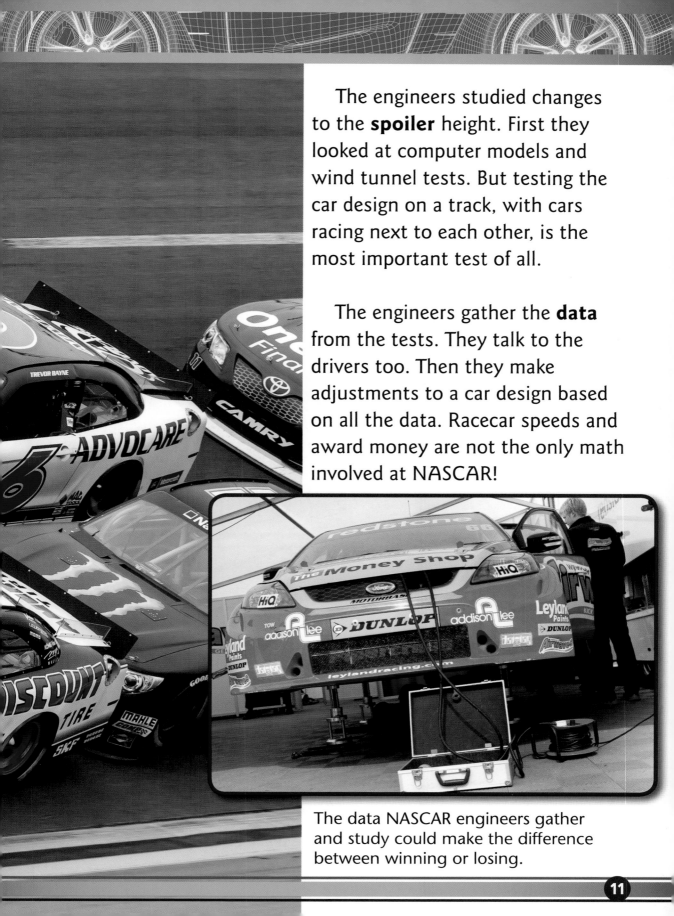

The engineers studied changes to the **spoiler** height. First they looked at computer models and wind tunnel tests. But testing the car design on a track, with cars racing next to each other, is the most important test of all.

The engineers gather the **data** from the tests. They talk to the drivers too. Then they make adjustments to a car design based on all the data. Racecar speeds and award money are not the only math involved at NASCAR!

The data NASCAR engineers gather and study could make the difference between winning or losing.

Building Better Cars

People use cars every day. They get people safely to school and soccer practice. With **GPS**, they guide the way to a vacation spot. But who are the brains behind the design of all the cars on the road? Automotive engineers! Many engineers have loved cars since they were kids and now get paid to play with them.

GPS technology points the way from one place to the next.

Car buyers want new improvements every year, so engineers are always thinking ahead. It wasn't long ago that a radio was the only form of entertainment in a vehicle. Now, there are ways to upload a playlist from your mobile device, watch a movie, or browse the Internet!

Engineers improve the technology and design of new cars.

The design of a car, including its weight and dimensions, affect how fast it goes and how it reacts in different conditions. You can see for yourself when you build some cars from Legos®.

Construct some Lego® cars with different shapes and weights. Take them for a spin: on the floor, up a ramp, or over bumps. How is each car suited to racing or carrying heavy loads over rocky roads?

The body of a car can be long and sleek or short and sturdy. Engineers turn a car design sketch into a detailed **blueprint**. They think about how the car will look, whether it will be safe, and what the building materials will cost.

There are also engineers who work on special **features**, such as rear-view cameras or motion-controlled trunk locks. With so many exciting possibilities, automotive engineers can have quite a unique career.

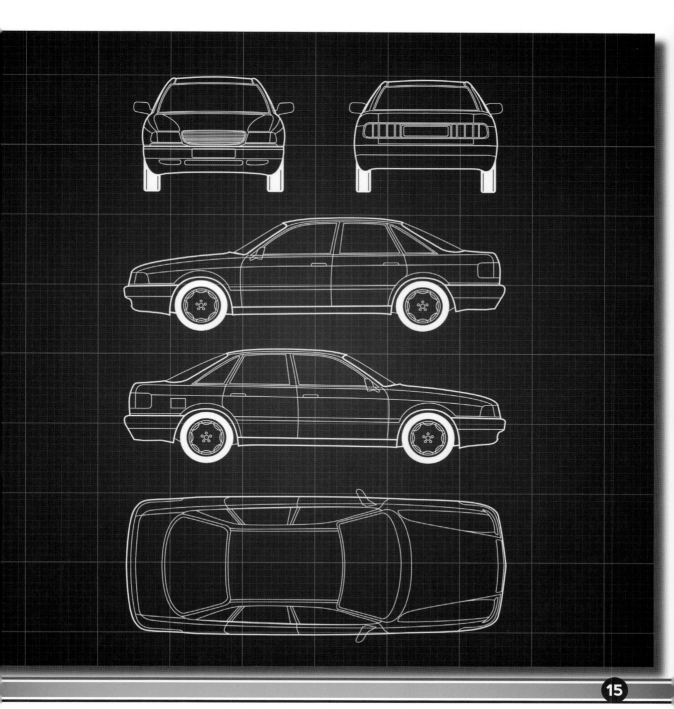

Real STEM Job: *Noise and Vibration Engineer*

Turn on a car and you'll probably hear the familiar rumbling and humming of the engine. But some car engineers have designed electric cars with very quiet electric motors. Passengers like the quiet, but it makes an engineer's job harder. Without the background noise of a typical engine, sounds from tires and wind can be heard.

To solve this problem, engineers place microphones in different areas inside the car. These microphones pick up unwanted sounds. Then, the car's audio system plays back opposite sounds to cancel them out!

Microphones placed inside a car are part of the car's noise control system.

This technology not only drowns out the sounds, but it also means that the car needs less sound-proofing material. With less material, the car weighs less and can get better gas mileage.

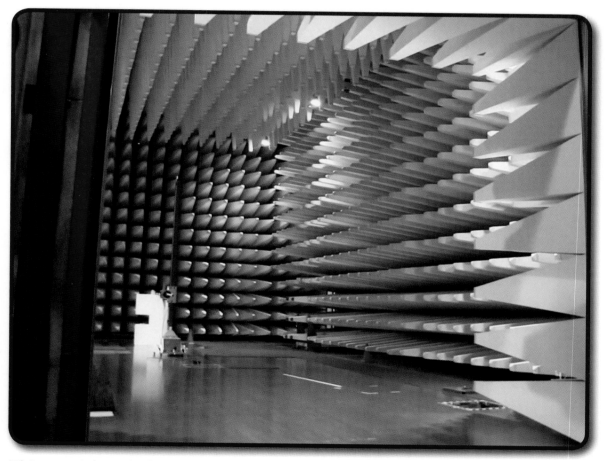

This special room has walls that absorb all sounds. It is the perfect place for engineers to study and test noise reduction in cars.

Using STEM to Solve a Mystery

Although traveling in a car is quite safe, car accidents do happen. Sometimes, police and scientists need to find out what caused a crash. Accident **reconstruction** experts will recreate the crash.

These experts are called to the scene as soon as the accident happens. They take measurements of the damage. Then they use computer programs and math formulas to find out what happened. How fast were the cars moving at impact? Were seat belts worn and would they have helped? Did the driver use the brakes? Experts can answer these questions and more.

A scientist takes exact measurements after an accident.

STEM in Action!

To find the energy of a moving car, you can use multiplication. Follow this equation:

$$E = \tfrac{1}{2} mv^2$$

What do those letters mean?

Energy = $\tfrac{1}{2}$ mass of the car × car velocity^2

To solve the equation, follow the order of operations: parentheses, **exponent**, multiply, divide, add, subtract.

If the car has a mass of 3,000 pounds and is going 50 miles per hour, plug these numbers into the equation to find how much energy it had.

Energy = $\tfrac{1}{2}$ × 3,000 pounds × (50 miles per hour)^2
= 1,500 pounds × 2,500 miles per hour
= 3,750,000

Many scientists who study crashes are also animators. They make 3-D computer movies of the crash! They use the data from the crash site to create the animation. This technology is useful when a judge or an insurance company needs help figuring out who caused the crash.

Real STEM Job: *Accident Reconstruction Engineer*

   A driver lost control of his car while going around a curve. He swerved off the road and hit a telephone pole. Unfortunately, he was badly hurt.

   The driver's family says that the road was badly paved and that the curve was dangerous. They say the county is responsible for the crash. The county calls in the accident reconstruction engineer.

   The engineer recreates the crash on paper. First, the engineer calculates that the driver had been going very fast. The engineer also discovers that the car left the pavement, causing the driver to lose control. Based on the scientist's data, the judge rules that the roadway and the curve are not dangerous.

Engineers use measurements from a crash site to understand how the crash happened

Building Greener Cars

Each year, scientists design more and more cars with **green** technology. For example, makers of **hybrid cars** design smaller, more efficient engines. These engines use less fuel, so hybrid cars make less pollution.

Some engineers design systems that capture energy when the brakes are used. The energy is stored in the battery and used later.

Hybrid cars cost less to run and are better for the environment.

Are there alternatives to gasoline? You bet. Chemists study biofuels made from plants, such as soybeans and corn, or from used cooking oil from a fast-food restaurant!

Since they are made from renewable plants, biofuels are friendly to the environment. They also give off fewer air pollutants than gasoline.

Soybeans are one source of energy for biofuels.

STEM Fast Fact:

Some scientists study how to turn sewage sludge into fuel! All the waste and water that goes down a drain goes to a water treatment plant. The sludge is removed and given to energy companies. That's one good way to make use of waste!

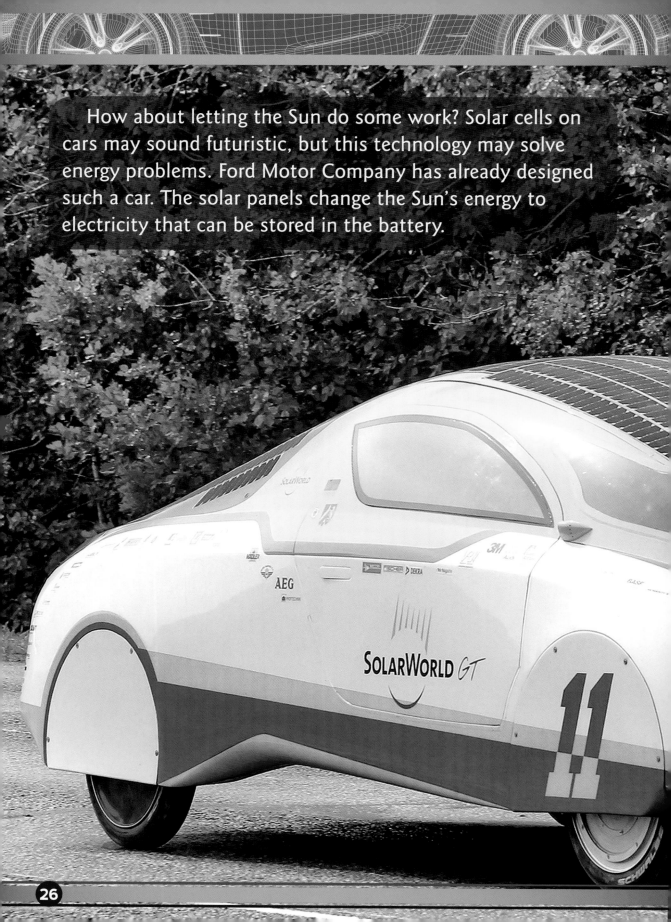

How about letting the Sun do some work? Solar cells on cars may sound futuristic, but this technology may solve energy problems. Ford Motor Company has already designed such a car. The solar panels change the Sun's energy to electricity that can be stored in the battery.

STEM in Action!

Some chemists use soybeans to make biofuel.

Suppose there are 40 bushels of soybeans harvested from one acre. And every bushel of soybeans produces 1.5 gallons of biofuel.

How many gallons of biofuel are produced per acre of soybean?

40 bushels × 1.5 gallons
= 60 gallons per acre

The solar cells on the roof of this car collect energy from the Sun.

STEM Spotlight: Using Oranges to Make Greener Tires

Material scientists are chemists. They look at the way **molecules** are combined in a material, such as rubber or plastic. Then they study how those combinations make a material more flexible, brittle, or durable. Material scientists have a new tire combination to make tires better for the environment. It uses an unusual ingredient: fruit!

The tire contains natural rubber and oil from orange peels. The oil reduces friction between the tire and the road, so the car gets better gas mileage. When the car is going around turns, heat softens the tire to give it better traction, or grip, on the road.

Safety First

Seat belts and air bags keep you safe in a car. But how do we know they work so well? Scientists put their math and science skills to use when they work to keep drivers safe.

Safety engineers test cars using computer crash **simulations** and crash test dummies. They gather data on the force a crash test dummy felt during a crash. Car makers can change their car designs based on the tests.

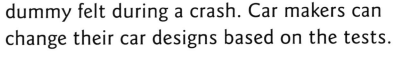

Crash test dummies help engineers design cars for safety.

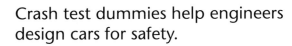

Wouldn't it be great to avoid an accident in the first place? Engineers are designing devices that can tell when a car is too close to another car or a person outside. Then automatic brakes stop the car to avoid an accident.

STEM Fast Fact: General Motors has a family of 200 crash test dummies! After many years of service, some crash test dummies make it to a museum. You can see one for yourself at the Smithsonian National Museum of American History.

STEM in Action!

Safety engineers also work on things like the car frame. They design it so that when a car crashes, the force on the car is spread out.

Let's see how this works.

Put on one high-heeled shoe and one sneaker. Go outside and stand on soft ground, such as grass or wet soil. Which shoe sinks into the ground more?

When all your body weight is resting in the smaller base of a high-heeled shoe, it sinks deeper into the soil. That's because there is more force in that small area. The sneaker, on the other hand, spreads the force over a larger area. You can see how spreading force out causes less damage to a surface.

The frame of a 2015 Chevy Corvette Stingray is built for both safety and sleek design.

What if a car driver's seat could vibrate to warn him that he was about to crash? That would be like a tap on the shoulder to say, "Watch out!" This is just one technology that engineers are building to make cars safer. What future things might you build?

STEM Spotlight: Meet the Crash Test Dummies

Strapped into the seat and barreling toward a wall, crash test dummies feel no pain. But the sensors strapped to their bodies collect important data that engineers study to make cars safer. Crash test dummies can send data 10,000 times per second!

Today's crash test dummies come in all sizes. They model adults, teens, toddlers, and newborns. Their skeletons are made of steel, and they are covered with rubber, vinyl, and foam. Some dummies have plastic bones and rubber rib cages that act more like the bones and bodies of people.

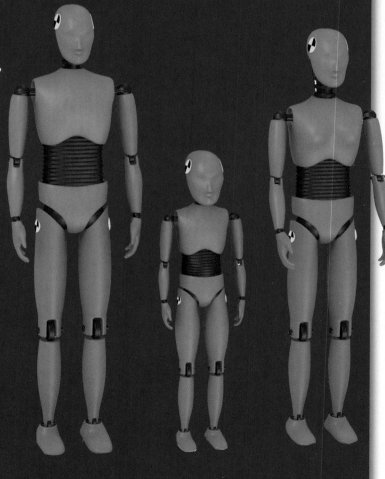

Building a Self-Driving Car

Automakers plan to soon sell cars that can drive themselves! Scientists use robotics to build driverless cars that can communicate with other cars and objects on the road.

When people drive, they watch the road, press the gas, steer, and brake as needed. Scientists are writing computer programs so that the robotic car takes in the same information as a real driver.

Roof-mounted **lasers**, computer vision, and GPS gather information to tell the car what is going on around it. When the car knows what is around it, the vehicle knows when to turn, stop, or speed up.

Volkswagen Automotive
Innovation Laboratory

Powered by D___

STANFORD
UNIVERSITY

A research initiative of the Volkswagen Group,
Electronics Research Laboratory and Stanford University

STEM in Action!

Engineers who write the computer programs for self-driving cars have to break simple tasks into dozens of small steps. To get an idea of how careful they need to be, try writing a "computer program," or a set of step-by-step instructions, for how to accomplish a task.

Write instructions for a friend to make a peanut butter and jelly sandwich. At first, it may seem like a simple task: Take two pieces of bread, smear with peanut butter and jelly, and slap them together! But each step can be broken down into more specific steps. You might want to start with "open a jar of peanut butter." But, what do you need to do before that? First you need to go to the kitchen, open the cabinet, reach in, and grasp the jar of peanut butter.

How many steps do you come up with? Can your friend break some of these steps into even smaller ones?

The engineers are designing these vehicles to be safer and help get rid of traffic problems. They would allow blind people to drive in some situations. These future cars could even drive themselves to get gas or an oil change!

There is room for two in this urban electric concept car. The EN-V can be either self-driven or operated by a driver.

STEM Spotlight: Google Robot Car

Google is the first place many people think of when searching online. Google is full of engineers and mathematicians. Some of them are building a self-driving robot car.

Some Google scientists use self-driving cars to get to work every day! The cars are still in the testing phase, though. They need a person sitting in the driver's seat to take over the driving during some maneuvers. An all-seeing spinning laser on the car's roof surveys the road as it heads to the office. Kind of a cool way to start the day, right?

The Future of Car Technology

Cars are now safer, sleeker, and more fuel-efficient. They have more options than ever before, and scientists never stop trying to improve them. They may even be driving themselves soon!

Biofuels, new building materials, and hybrid cars will help cars be more fuel efficient with less impact on the environment. With so much new technology every year, mathematicians, engineers, and scientists will continue to find exciting careers working with cars.

STEM Job Fact Sheets

Automotive Engineer

Important Skills: Mathematics, Critical Thinking, Science

Important Knowledge: Mathematics, Engineering, Vehicle Design, Car Mechanics

College Major: Physics, Mechanical Engineering, Electrical Engineering, Industrial Engineering, Computer Engineering

Median Salary: $82,000

Accident Reconstruction Engineer

Important Skills: Computer Proficiency, Critical Thinking, Car Design, Photography, Evidence Analysis, Report Writing, Strong Communication Skills

Important Knowledge: Criminology, Law, Physics, Mathematics, Engineering

College Major: Criminology, Physics, Engineering

Median Salary: $65,000

Biofuel Scientist

Important Skills: Chemistry, Biology, Physics, Laboratory Skills, Data Analysis

Important Knowledge: Biochemistry, Automotive Engines, Plant Science

College Major: Chemistry, Physics, Biology

Median Salary: $65,000

Crash Safety Engineer

Important Skills: Math, Physics, Computer Proficiency, Statistics
Important Knowledge: Math, Computers, Problem-Solving
College Major: Mechanical Engineering
Median Salary: $72,000

Electric Car or Hybrid Car Engineer

Important Skills: Research, Computer Proficiency, Mechanics
Important Knowledge: Mathematics, Physics, Engine Design, Electricity
College Major: Mechanical Engineering, Physics
Median Salary: $80,580

NASCAR Engineer

Important Skills: Math, Electrical Engineering, Auto Racing, Computer Proficiency
Important Knowledge: Computer Science, Mathematics
College Major: Electrical Engineering, Mechanical Engineering
Median Salary: $75,000

Glossary

blueprint (BLOO-print): a technical drawing of a design plan

data (DEY-tuh): facts and statistics

exponent (EK-spoh-nuhnt): a raised number over another number in mathematics; indicates how many times to multiply the lower number by itself

features (FEE-churz): something special added to help get someone to buy the item

GPS (GEE-PEE-ES): a navigation tool used to tell a position on Earth and to give directions to a specific location

green (GREEN): good for the environment

hybrid cars (HY-brid kahrz): vehicles with two sources of power, such as gasoline and electricity

lasers (LAY-zurz): devices that send out a beam of light

molecules (MAH-le-kyools): the smallest amount of a substance that still contains the characteristics of that substance

reconstruction (ree-kuhn-STRUHK-shun): the act of building something again

simulations (sim-yoo-LAY-shuns): something that is built to look, act, or move like something else so that it can be studied closely

spoiler (SPOI-lur): a car part built to prevent air drag along the body of a car; it "spoils" air drag that could slow the car down

Index

Show What You Know

1. What types of technologies are scientists using to make more environmentally-friendly cars?
2. How does a self-driving car know where it is going?
3. How do NASCAR racers use scientists and mathematicians to win races?
4. How does an engineer reduce the noise a passenger hears inside a car?
5. Why do crash test dummies come in different sizes?

Websites to Visit

www.coolsciencecareers.rice.edu

www.engineergirl.org

www.tryscience.org

About the Author

Jane Katirgis has always loved science, which led her to a BS degree in biology and an MS degree in environmental science. She is a children's science book editor and author, and also an Etsy shop owner. She currently drives a Subaru Crosstrek. Jane lives in New Jersey with her husband, John, and their four egg-laying chickens.

Meet The Author!
www.meetREMauthors.com

www.rourkeeducationalmedia.com

PHOTO CREDITS: Cover © Svariophoto, Supergenijalac, andresrimaging; Title page © Mikhail Bakunovich; page 4-5 © Andrey Yurlov, page 5 inset © Corepics VOF; page 6 © Doug James, page 7 © Andresr, top photo © Visionsi; page 9 top © Beelde Photography, bottom © Anatoliy Lukich; page 10-11 © Action Sports Photography, page 11 © Steve Mann; page 12 © AntonioDiaz, page 13 © Rafal Olechowski; page 14 and 15 © Mikhail Bakunovich; page 16 © DmitriMaruta, page 17 © Binarysequence; page 18-19 © conrado, page 19 © Jack Dagley Photography; page 20-21 © Tom Plesnik, page 21 inset © Denis Rozhnovsky, image on computer screen © Stanracz; page 22-23 © Tim Large, page 23 inset © Jack Dagley Photography; page 24-25 © Michael Shake, page 25 inset © JIANG HONGYAN; page 26-27 © Art Konovalov; page 28-29 © supergenijalac, page 28 inset © domnitsky; page 30 top © Ken Schulze, bottom page 30 © 3drenderings, page 31 © Robert Crum; page 32-33 © Darren Brode; page 34 © Master3D, page 35 © 3drenderings; page 36-37 © Steve Jurvetson, page 39 © segwaysocial2; page 40-41 © Steve Jurvetson; page 42-43 © Darren Brode

Edited by: Jill Sherman

Cover design by: Tara Raymo
Interior design by: Nicola Stratford   nicolastratford.com

Library of Congress PCN Data

STEM Jobs with Cars / Jane Katirgis
(STEM Jobs You'll Love)
ISBN 978-1-62717-702-3 (hard cover)
ISBN 978-1-62717-824-2 (soft cover)
ISBN 978-1-62717-938-6 (e-Book)
Library of Congress Control Number: 2014935495

Printed in the United States of America, North Mankato, Minnesota

Also Available as:

ROURKE'S
e-Books